... SONGS OF THE '70s

Collection for Young Voices
Arranged by Alan Billingsley

T0055822

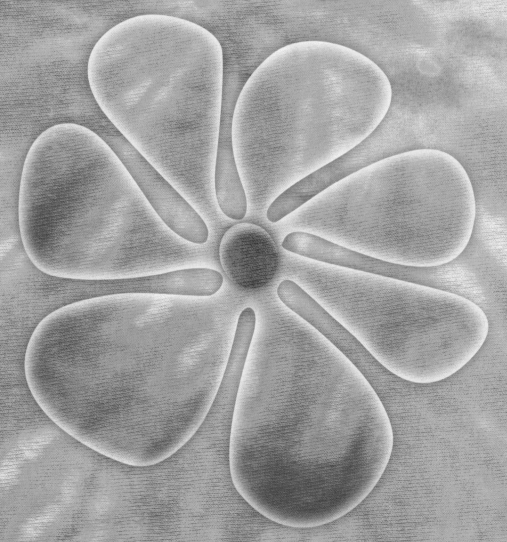

Visit Hal Leonard Online at
www.halleonard.com

I JUST WANT TO CELEBRATE

Words and Music by
NICK ZESSES and DINO FEKARIS
Arranged by ALAN BILLINGSLEY

I just want to cel - e - brate, yeah, yeah, an - oth - er day of liv - in', yeah!

I just want_ to cel - e - brate_ an - oth - er day_ of liv - in'.

I just want_ to cel - e - brate_ an - oth - er day_ of life!

Don't let it all_ get you down, no, no.

slight vocal fall on each "round"

Don't let it turn you a - round, round, round.

Well I can't be both - ered with sor - row, and I

can't be both - ered with hate. I'm us - in' up my time by feel - in fine

ev - 'ry day. That's why I'm tell - in' you, I just want to cel - e - brate an -

I'VE GOT THE MUSIC IN ME

Words and Music by BIAS BOSHELL
Arranged by ALAN BILLINGSLEY

I got the mu-sic in___ me. I got the mu-sic in___ me.

They say that life is a cir-cle, but that___ ain't the way___ that I found___ it.

I'm gon-na move in a straight___ line, keep-in' my feet firm-

I got the mu-sic in__ me. I got the mu-sic in__ me. I got the mu-sic in__ me.

Feel funk-y. Feel good.

Gon-na tell__ you, I'm__ in the neigh-bor-hood. Gon-na fly__ like a bird__

__ on the wing. Hold on__ to your hat,__ hon-ey. Sing, sing, sing, sing!

13

I got the mu - sic in___ me. I got the mu - sic in___ me. I got the mu - sic in me.

I got the mu - sic in___ me. I got the mu - sic in___ me.

I got the mu - sic in me. I got the mu - sic___ in me.

LEAN ON ME

Words and Music by BILL WITHERS
Arranged by ALAN BILLINGSLEY

* Optional: add some singers an octave below

For no one can fill those of your needs that you won't let show. You just call on me broth-er when you need a hand. We all need some-bod-y to lean on. I just might have a prob-lem that you'll un-der-stand. We all need some-bod-y to lean on. Lean on me,

clap on the offbeats through mea. 34

end claps

might have a prob-lem that you'll un-der-stand. We all need some-bod-y to lean

on. We all need some-bod-y to lean on.

Call me, call me, call me,

call me, call me.

OLD TIME ROCK & ROLL

Words and Music by GEORGE JACKSON
and THOMAS E. JONES III
Arranged by ALAN BILLINGSLEY

melody in lower notes [53] *(add claps on beats 2 & 4 to end)*

drums only

I re-mi-nisce a-bout the days of old,___ with that old___ time (ah) rock and roll. Still like that old___ time (ah) rock and roll. That kind of mu-sic just___ soothes the soul.___ I re-mi-nisce a-bout the days of old,___ with that old_____ time (ah) rock and roll.

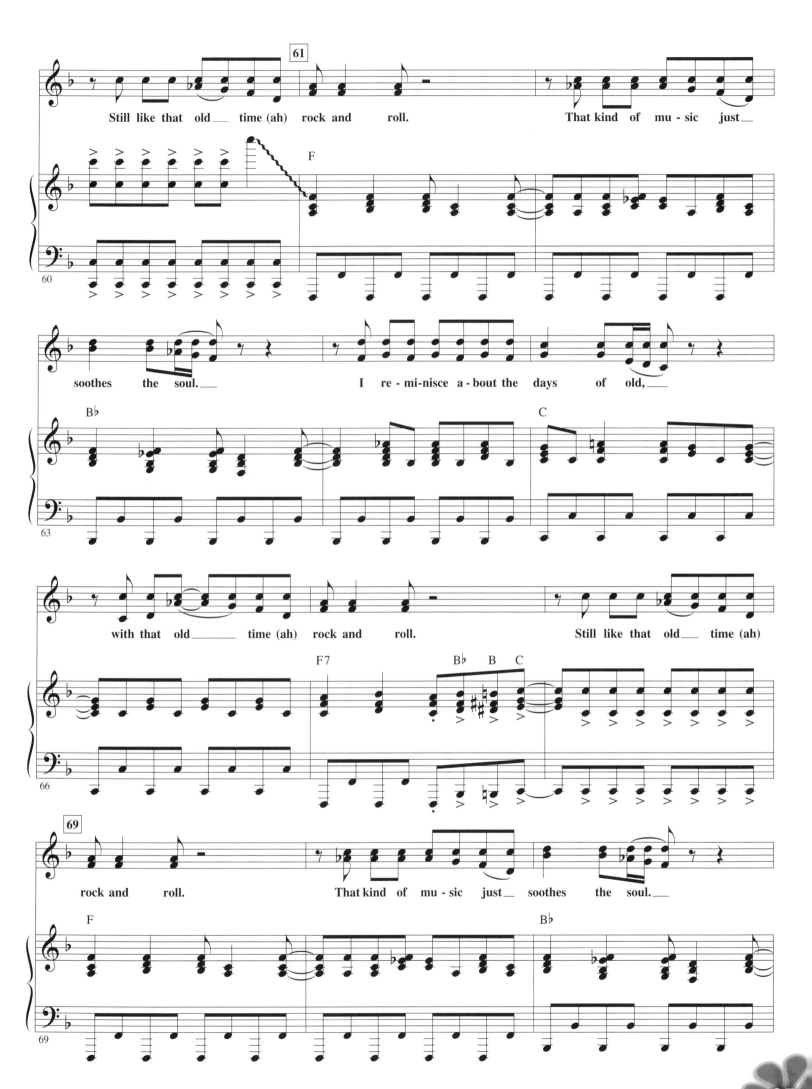

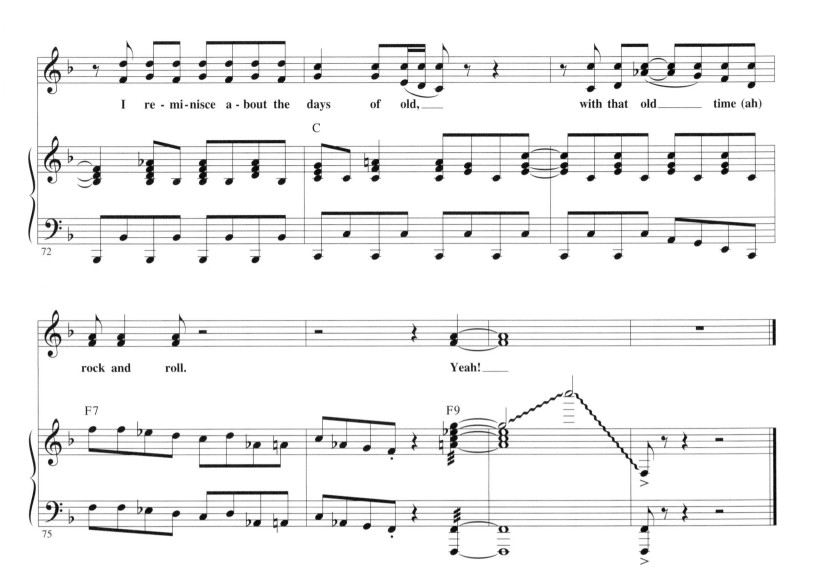

I re - mi - nisce a - bout the days of old,_____ with that old_____ time (ah)

rock and roll. Yeah!_____

YOU'VE GOT A FRIEND

Words and Music by CAROLE KING
Arranged by ALAN BILLINGSLEY

Y.M.C.A.

Words and Music by JACQUES MORALI,
HENRI BELOLO and VICTOR WILLIS
Arranged by ALAN BILLINGSLEY